D0595539

Lumina and New Lumina

Happy Birthday
Love
Katie
04/08/2019

ADRIENNE VON SPEYR

Lumina
and
New Lumina

TRANSLATED BY ADRIAN WALKER

IGNATIUS PRESS   SAN FRANCISCO

Original German edition:
Lumina und Neue Lumina
© 1969 by Johannes Verlag, Einsiedeln
Second, enlarged edition

Cover art:
Two doves drinking from a fountain.
Mosaic. Early Christian, ca. A.D. 425
Mausoleum of Galla Placidia, Ravenna, Italy
© Cameraphoto Arte, Venice/Art Resource, New York

Cover design by Roxanne Mei Lum

© 2008 by Ignatius Press, San Francisco
All rights reserved
ISBN 978-1-58617-222-0
Library of Congress Control Number 2007928637
Printed in the United States of America ∞

Contents

Prefatory Note

Christianity is either love of God, or it is nothing. As for everything else—do not even the pagans do that, too? Before telling the Parable of the Good Samaritan, Christ asks the scribe to recite the Great Commandment with which the Old Covenant stands and falls. "You have answered rightly. Do this, and you will live." Elsewhere, in Matthew, Christ himself recites it in answer to the question of which is the weightiest commandment of the Law. That there is "a second like it"—to love "your neighbor as yourself"—is the consequence the New Testament draws from the Word of God. The creature embraces its Creator (who—once he lovingly elects the creature—becomes its covenant Lord) with the love of its whole heart, whole soul, and whole mind. And now my neighbor is included in that love. For God himself loves this neighbor as himself, and he became a neighbor, my neighbor, in order to prove it. The second commandment cannot be had without the first; it is what spills over when the first is fulfilled; if you invert the order, under whatever pretext, you are bound in good logic to give up Christianity.

It is precisely when God becomes man that he also becomes recognizable as the archetypal Love, which is triune in its very nature. Being (reality, the primordial ground of all things) and love coincide; from now on, to exist in harmony with being means: to love. Not just by contemplating, like the Indians and Greeks, but with a burning need to love archetypal Love in return. With a burning need to love personally, and that means: by praying, just as Jesus prayed, with the prayers of the Old Covenant on his lips; and just as everyone whose life has shone with Christian fire has prayed in his footsteps for the last two thousand years. And to love personally also means: with one's whole existence, stripped of self for Christian engagement, in mission to one's fellowmen and to the world, in order that both may be changed according to God's mind and spirit. "Political theology", they say nowadays. Yes, of course, but not just with actions. Rather, *beyond* actions, with the engagement of one's life, to the point of performing the supreme action (which makes sense only as a Christian gesture): substitutionary suffering. Passion does not replace action, because passion is God's most active engagement on behalf of love. It does not replace action, because God uses it to initiate the Christian, who would do more for love if he could, into the mysteries of a reality whose overflowing efficacy lies beyond the Christian's own capacities.

Even as a small child, Adrienne von Speyr (1902–

1967), daughter of an old Basel family, wanted to become a doctor to help her fellowmen. Though she faced both an extremely hard fight against familial resistance and a series of illnesses that threatened to bring her plans to nought, she finally did achieve her goal. From childhood, she knew instinctively that she could truly help her neighbor, both professionally and humanly, only if she was in full harmony with God, and she failed to find this harmony in her conventional Protestant environment. She was in search of the unreserved openness to God that—after her conversion in 1940—she found in the sacrament of confession; she was in search of the union with the incarnate Lord that she was to receive from the Holy Mass; above all, she was in search of the permission to disappear completely into the objectivity of mission and the self-dispossession attendant on it. This permission was the gift she received in the Church, both as institution and as Christ's "body" and "bride".

After a number of years devoted to an exhausting professional practice, Adrienne faced decades during which illness increasingly prevented any outside work. In moments of leisure, she dictated meditations on the Bible, particularly on the Johannine corpus; between 1947 and the time of this writing, thirty-four volumes have appeared, and, contrary to the assertions of the occasional bookseller, they are by no means out of print. She spent her nights almost entirely in prayer and her afternoons quietly embroidering or (as she began to go blind) knitting. During such hours she would from time to time pull out a notebook and write down one of the thoughts that the reader will find in what follows; she then stuck the pages in the desk drawer where they were discovered after her death. In their artless concision, they offer distillations of the essence of her thinking, praying, and being.

Why publish them? Because we rarely hear today their native echo of the inmost mystery of Christianity. Because the paradox of ardent sobriety that they display bears the mark of authenticity. Perhaps simply in order to show that such things still exist.[1]

Hans Urs von Balthasar

---

[1] An autobiography of Adrienne von Speyr (*Aus meinem Leben*) was published in the fall of 1968 by Johannes Verlag, Einsiedeln [translated by Mary Emily Hamilton and Dennis D. Martin and included in the volume *My Early Years* (San Francisco: Ignatius Press, 1995)]. The same publisher has also brought out my *Erster Blick auf Adrienne von Speyr* (1968) [translated by Antje Lawry and Sr. Sergia Englund, O.C.D., as *First Glance at Adrienne von Speyr* (San Francisco: Ignatius Press, 1981)], as well as by far the largest number of her works. Her posthumous writings comprise twelve volumes (some of them double volumes) and are now being prepared for publication under my editorship; they contain the most significant things she said. The word "lumina" that appears in the title is used in the older literature to mean short "insights", especially ones written down after being received in contemplative prayer.

On the Second Edition

We add a second loose selection from the abundance of notes for unwritten books, aphorisms, and fragments left by Adrienne von Speyr. Like the first, it obeys no tight structure. Unlike the first, it begins with the personal, continues on through the objective, and finally issues in prayer.

HANS URS VON BALTHASAR

Lumina

I

Love of self is love that measures itself; love of neighbor is love that gives itself away. The only thing you can say about love of God is: it leaves behind scorched earth.

Anyone who knows the fullness of the light should not live in the twilight for the sake of thrift.

There are things that the understanding cannot grasp: they are too big for it, because their measure is love.

Love has no beginning, since before it became concrete, it was already present in the attitude of readiness.

When we make our own calculations, we need so many numbers and factors that any mistake is possible. The Lord's calculation boils down to love.

Ultimate audacity: to want to love a person—to say nothing of one's neighbor!—as God loves him.

Christian love means two things at once: to recognize the Lord in one's neighbor and to recognize one's neighbor in the Lord.

The first step in learning to love others is the attempt to understand them.

To get or to understand people always means: to look at them from God's angle, from the point of view communicated through Him. It is not a science, but a pure grace.

To love a friend in the right way can mean: to be able to prefer others to him in the Lord.

When someone dies, people often think: "If only he could still speak." The real opinion of the living is something people are only rarely curious to find out.

Faith is a force, one so powerful that it cannot tolerate anything next it. How weak in faith we are: we are constantly letting things outside of God take up space in us!

There is just as little center in what one has experienced as there is in virtually any living thing. It is a grace of God that, in the end, even life itself remains without a center.

Being and being Christian are an absolute unity for the believer. Trying to separate or even to delineate the two would be to give up living.

Faith enables Christian hope to be more than mere expectation and to become at every moment an immediate embodiment of love.

Only faith can keep what hope promises.

Christian hope is a vessel in which faith lives; love carries it.

For someone who believes in God's love, there is nothing too paradoxical to be believed.

When the Lord communicates a truth to us, its truthfulness obviously lies not just in the means He uses to communicate it, but also in Him. In the same way, then, a truth that a believer draws on faith to communicate must be true both in him and in the Lord.

We must leave every moment to Providence; then we also know there is no such thing as "the meaningless".

We can never fully abstract from our good works, because, no matter how small and imperfect they are, they come from God even before they are performed; we must thank Him for them and, once they are done, return them completely to Him and place them at His disposal.

Let us make a rosary of our life, placing every incident in it, and offering up our daily cares with a quick Ave Maria.

There is only one thing I need to live: love. Lord, take only love, so that I will not always give You only what I have left over and so that *I* may finally stop living: may *You* live.

Certain divisions are necessary in order to reveal the unity of the whole: but this is not a matter of breaking atoms out of a molecule formed by their convergence.

Right love is steady in its indivisibility. It is so indivisible, in fact, that in the end there is no longer any clearly discernible boundary-marker between love given and love received. Even more: this unity also includes humility. This humility is not dispersed, and it alone enables love to become what it already was in the beginning: a gift of the Lord having a definite form.

Enlarging the circle does not mean merely drawing as many distant points around it as possible, but rather drawing all these points, wherever they may lie, into the communion of the one circle.

Unless you have some sense of God's mercy, you cannot possibly say anything about man's sufferings.

Our faith is meant to be strong enough to understand everything: even hatred and unbelief. Then we will love the haters and the unbelievers and ask God to do His work.

There is nothing more at rest than love, because it is security itself; and yet it never stands still, because the need for communication is inherent in it, and expansiveness is part of its being. In this sense, love is restless.

The people whom we most respect are perhaps the very ones who are most in need of love.

Love can mean: making room in yourself for the understanding your loved one has, even when you do not understand it.

The suffocation of the message in the incomprehension of others.

The more mysterious God is to you, the closer He is to you.

We often kneel, not in order to petition or to express an inner attitude, but only in order to announce that we have arrived. But where have we arrived? Merely at the place from which God wants to push us farther along. The destination always becomes a point of departure; the fact that we have arrived means at most the beginning of a new journey.

Love has so infinitely many possibilities. How amazing, then, it is for us to know that all of them are embraced in this one word.

Whoever wants to love is better knowing nothing than too much.

Once a scientific question is settled, it remains interesting and alive only if it draws attention to new questions; every conclusion is meant as a transition to a new beginning.

Only when you are familiar with silence have you learned to speak; what you have to say can ripen only in silence.

In Christ silence often has a more long-lasting effect than speech.

It is not just the art of giving that one is supposed to possess, but also the art of being able to receive and accept.

God has created the sex act as a sort of symbol of the deep meaning hidden in every authentic gift: its fruitfulness demonstrates itself only with time.

There is already so much grace in a Christian body. Can you imagine how much grace there is in a soul?

Joy is not only a public profession. It is above all a state, and the same is true of humility and faith.

It is never the case that God's love *has* opened up in us; it is always in the act of opening up.

II

There is perhaps just one criterion for measuring love, and it lies in obedience. This strikes me every time I see how children relate to their parents. But is it just as evident in the way we relate to God?

A ring with a visible seam is imperfect. Even more imperfect is an obedience with any hint of compulsion.

On the stage, a person has to learn to be someone else; in life, he has to learn to be himself, which seems to be considerably more difficult: to discover his mission and to live within the core of it.

One isolated blow still does not have the full effect; it could just be a matter of chance. Only when the blows start repeating do I notice that they are actually intended for me. How often does God have to call before I listen?!

Prayer and obedience should become a unity in us, and this unity should be so perfect that the two things cannot be separated. In order to become one, they need to join together; in order to join together, they at least have to exist in the first place. Do prayer and obedience really exist in my case, if only for one moment of every day?

We have said: "We are giving up everything", and by that we meant: "We want only You." That word "only" still reflects the measure of our covetousness, but that word "You" reflects the measure of Your infinite mercy.

A lot of people have an itch to throw themselves completely into something; they are always volunteering to serve some cause, but once they have taken the full measure of it, they lose interest. If instead of that they just put themselves at God's service, when do you suppose they would ever finish taking the full measure of *that*?

Everyone wants to be a father or a son, but no one wants to be a grandfather or a grandson.

Cutting one tie always means getting tied to something new that is usually not yet tied up. Resolving to be unloosed from God rarely leaves you loose, and it never resolves your problem.[1]

---

[1] Ent-Bindung besagt stets Bindung zu Neuem, meist noch Unverbundenem. Loslösung von Gott is selten ein Los, nie eine Lösung.

Every step along the path can mean a disappointment; after all, no step can be the last one on the way to the goal or even open up the whole view.

We are constantly falling into the temptation to give ourselves somewhat in the way that people give money, which is to say, within the limits of their own calculation. God grant us the grace to stop calculating once and for all, to give ourselves just as we are, provided we do it wholly and always more. What is in the purse is something He alone needs to know. And even that is not necessary.

Presents that cost money can be graded with the most amazing precision; there are infinite variations between a penny and a fortune, and each one of them can be turned into a gift. Love is something you give only when you give it whole, prodigally. So here there is just one possibility, and it contains every possibility.

The measure of service is what conveys an inkling of the possibility of freedom.

You live in us, Lord. Let us become nothing but a dwelling. We tidy it up, doing our part as best we can until God arrives. But then our attention has to be for the guest, and only very, very secondarily for the dwelling.

Every Yes in the Catholic sense is something whole, something without any conditions; it promises more than it can keep. So the Lord must take charge of this Yes and fulfill it, so the fulfillment therefore necessarily contains much more than the promise could suggest.

When small children are with their father, they do not keep asking questions, nor do they constantly ask for something else; they may be a little better behaved than usual in their playing; they tell him what they are doing, and they have the feeling, which is probably never completely expressed, that the tower they are building will turn out taller with a grown-up nearby than if they were alone. Then they ask their father to tell them how things were before, and they never tire of finding out everything they can grasp; they want to become like him; they look for points of contact, make comparisons; they try in their very modest way to imitate their father a little.

Father, give us the grace to become like these little children. Do not let us constantly disturb the gift of Your presence with our demands. Let us learn instead to come closer and closer to You in the silence of prayer and to let You work, so that through You the task You give us may come into being and flourish.

If you are a believer, then you do not need to choose your path. The Lord will trace it out clearly enough for you. But that means: your path can change from day to day; it may not be necessary to travel down the entire stretch of road you have been shown. What is more, even though you saw the path, you often do not know where it is, and at the very least the surrounding landscape remains hidden from view.

We pray "Thy will be done" when it is necessary to accept, to decide, or to put up with something. And even more, even closer, when it is necessary to support *You*, to magnify Your power, to enable its accomplishment. This is how we share in Your work: when we do our part—even more by our prayer than by our action—to help Your will be done, however it may turn out. We do not only bow under it, then, but we are drawn into it; it becomes our willing, precisely because it is Yours.

You are quite at liberty to doubt, provided you keep alive the ability to cry out with Thomas "My lord and my God!" at the right time.

For every handmaid there comes the hour when she can cry out "Let it be to me according to Your will." And for me "Your will" means everything lying within the limits You have imposed on Yourself by Your Law, and so: everything lying within the Good. The Good, however, is absolute, and as such it has no boundaries. Its only boundaries are the ones separating it from evil, which by definition are not really boundaries within the compass of the Good itself. But no creature can live in the absolute. That is why You have delineated paths within the compass of the Good—which also means: within the compass of Your will—and have even delineated a particular path for each handmaid, regardless of how many of us there are. "Let it be to me according to Your will" finally means just one thing for us: Let me remain on the path You have already marked out for me. Not first seek this path, but remain on it. For if the path were still completely hidden, or had even been missed, the handmaid could no longer cry "Let it be to me according to Your will." The first symptom of being lost, in fact, is that one has already lost the ability to speak to You. The person who no longer prays has already lost You; a person who prays does not need to seek You, despite all his protestations. You have him already.

Just one thing I ask You, Lord: fill up my prayer with what belongs to You; let what belongs to me be submerged, and put in its place what belongs to You, which You can take from wherever You will: from Your days of tranquil earthly contentment, from the agony on the Mount of Olives, from the sufferings of the Cross, from Your incomprehensible procession from the Father in the Trinity, or from Your return to the Father—from wherever You will, so long as it belongs to You, not distorted by my weakenss, not inhibited by my sin, but only entering into Your eternal will.

Not my will, Lord. Not any more.

III

Conscience is nothing but interior knowledge bound up in God.

The core of the essential passes mostly through the inessential.

There are things that can be verified only in the Lord, verified not just in the Spirit whom He bestows, but also in the hour He gives and in no other.

Some wounds are only aggravated by balm and healed by the knife; there is no more salutary operation imaginable than the work of the sword that separates good from evil in the Spirit.

Before anyone starts pondering anything, his soul always needs first to be put into the state of love.

Any movement can become indecent if the eye that intercepts it interprets it that way.

It is impossible to write laws of freedom. By their nature they are so inflexible that they are at one and the same time obvious and impossible to follow—

that is, for sinful man, who is under the constant constraint of having to focus his knowledge exclusively on God's will.

To get used to things means merely to rob them of their deeper meaning. Here is an example: your Sunday best was once an ornament, but later you began using it for everyday wear. All it does now is perform a service; it no longer adorns you.

When you go into a shop with something particular in mind, you show no reluctance to buy the thing that fits just right. But when God offers you something, you walk right by either without attending to it or without accepting it. Is it maybe because the price-tag on His graces does not state clearly enough that they are completely gratis?

You can grant the devil certain powers in order to bind him. But what is a devil bound if not an effectual demonstration of the perfect freedom in God?

When the Lord says that He is the truth, He means something so absolute that no human comprehension or measurement is ever sufficient to grasp it. By contrast, the absoluteness of every technological truth lies within the grasp of our understanding, however clouded, and therefore lies beneath it. And so we are fully dispensed from having to bow before technology.

It may be all right for a scientific truth to be paired with pride. Christian truth, however, is inseparably united with humility.

That unattainable is attained you see in Christ; at every point He shows you His greatness by giving Himself to you as an example. If you think you can follow His example, however, He disappears, leaving you behind; He takes the greatness along with Him, and there is no question that you are the littleness.

You are not debarred from loving yourself, but love yourself as you do any of your neighbors, with humility and in the grace of the Lord. Try it, and then you will perhaps realize that it is precisely this you cannot do.

The more subjectivisms feed into the one subjectivism, the more man, who is always disposed to the subjective, tends to believe that he is finally dealing with true objectivity. This is the error of every age. Only the objective can lead to the objective. The subjective is an accident and has to be recognized as such, even when it opens new horizons and proves to be a side path that leads to truth.

God creates time and space. He places His action in them, and that is decisively important for understanding better: for getting an inkling of His infinity. The infinite does not begin in some unknown place. It is always starting here and now. This lays the groundwork for explaining God's omnipresence.

If you refused fullness to yesterday, you cannot expect it from today.

If I had ever had to think that something was my work, I would probably never have had another moment's rest in God.

I set about contemplating Your works: I was thirsty, and You gave me food; I grew astonished. I was hungry, and You offered me water; my know-it-all manner expanded. I was cold, and You sent me a gust of cold air; I grew agitated and wanted to correct You. I was getting more and more heated, and You wrapped me in blankets. Then I realized: it is not my needs that are supposed to be important to me; Yours are the only ones to which I should pay attention. Lord, take what is mine, and let it disappear completely and be replaced by what is Yours.

Penance is never a self-contained act, it is always just preparation. If it loses this quality, then it is simply misunderstood and would be better stopped.

Spiritual dispossession is probably never a onetime action. I voluntarily surrender to it, but then I derive from this very willingness a right to keep checking that what I left behind is still there, to play the owner, to try to save something. And this contraband that I smuggle in on the side is what the Lord inexorably demands.

Physical sufferings might not even be necessary if suffering souls did not have so many narcotics at their fingertips.

We have the tendency to process divine truths through our understanding and turn them into human ones. But God wills that everything that is divine should stay divine.

Worthiness and unworthiness are two extremes without a single point of contact; what objectively separates them exactly covers the distance that yawns between God and man.

The absolute can never take on real existence for us when what we call real existence is measured by our temporal condition and is supposed to prove itself inside it.

The sins of others can never become the measure of your own.

Since contemporary psychology refuses to have anything more in common with Christology, for the time being there can be no "psychology *and* faith", only "psychology *or* faith".

Is self-abandonment something so total that anything opposed to it does not weaken it but can only completely destroy it?

You want to abandon yourself? You had best refrain if you lack the strength to do it completely. There are works of art that should never be ventured if the artist lacks sufficient strength to achieve them fully. In the long run, a promise that always only promises becomes insufferable, both in art and in self-abandonment.

Most of the time you cannot distinguish the great from the small, and that is a good thing; otherwise, you would constantly choose, instead of praying; you would hesitate, instead of acting.

If there were just one possibility—either to do the good *or* to combat evil—man would have to opt for the first.

Evil words usually have a quicker effect than good ones. But good ones sometimes have a longer-lasting effect than evil ones.

True anger is a just and fine thing. Prayer serves as its crucible and purifies it. If it comes forth from prayer, such anger glows with all the more radiance, and it has only enhanced prayer's vitality. Unjust anger, however, fears prayer and dries it up.

One of the hardest things is to prove to man that something in his past was wrong. For what man fears most is that his present might start to wobble. We more easily admit the mistakes of today, because we think that we can improve them.

For the Christian, contrition actually comes before insight; in a certain sense, he first regrets his sin, and then insight grows out of contrition.

It does not matter what the persecutor looks like; often enough it is Christ Himself, hidden behind a set of human features, who is offering us His homeland. In that case, persecution is the supreme and ultimate expression of His love.

With most people it is only after their death that you find out whether their existence was life.

IV

The Lord's blood never congeals. It remains living and flows warm through all ages.

What flows out of the wound in the Lord's side flows, as it were, into us. It gives us the new blood and water for the resurrection of the flesh.

Baudelaire: "*Les nations n'ont de grands hommes que malgré elles.*"[1] You need only substitute "Church" for "nations" and "saints" for "men" in order to understand our situation!

You never know where true responsibility begins, but you have even less idea where it ends. It has many different faces, and none of them can be labeled false.

It is impossible to exercise any care of souls unless one has handed over the entire care of one's own soul to God.

Most people respond to one lack of peace with another. While the first one was interior, the second

---

[1] "Nations have great men only in spite of themselves."— TRANS.

one is exterior; it originates from the human urge to justify oneself, to demonstrate how certain one is inwardly. The Catholic Church contains probably the most striking examples of that.

Joylessness is perfectly capable of smothering the truth in intellectual work. Where may joylessness in theology yet bring Christ's Church?

If your neighbor has faith, you can help him in his faith. His path, however, remains in the Lord and belongs to Him. Do not try to change his path.

Everything the Lord gives and everything He takes is indivisible. He always has more to bestow, because He draws on a super-abundant reserve. In bestowing His gift, though, He gives it the look of a complete whole. Not only that, He actually makes it into a complete whole as well.

Of all men, priests are the ones most able to beget, because they have the word. The word, though, is God's seed and is uncounted.

The archetypal situation of the parents of new priests: they suppose their son is lost, and they find him again only in the Temple.

Something of the priest's consecration always works retroactively on the graces of his parents' matrimonial consecration: not just in order to strengthen them, but also to give them a sort of absolution.

Nothing can be compared with love. For the more I love the One, Jesus Christ, the more of my love becomes free for others, for every single one of those others. And yet, it is not my love for Him that generates new love, but just the other way around: His love for me.

The more love one receives, the poorer one is. The more love one gives away, the richer one becomes. Wealth finally becomes limitless, in fact, only when it has become naked poverty.

Every young couple that comes together believes they are the first people in the world to have discovered love, and they feel it as a burden that others know about love. Those who love God, however, are grateful to know they are not alone in this love; they feel they are greatly enriched by others.

We should regard every celebration of other people as our own. The reason we so rarely celebrate is that we are constantly seeking celebrations of our own.

On the Cross the Lord suffered for all our sins; in confession, therefore, we need to show only the sins for which we ourselves are responsible, the ones for which He has to suffer anew, so to speak.

In the confessional we would all like to be considered not quite *compos mentis*.

When we sin, we think we are geniuses; when we confess, we know we are idiots.

A Christian who refused to die after confession would be unworthy of life.

A person's refusal to communicate out of fear that he is not pure enough to receive the Lord can be a lack of love. After all, the Lord's radiance shines infinitely over everything; any attempt at comparison is arrogance; let us allow Him to give us His gifts, even if we do not have anything to give in return. That might actually be the beginning of love.

The anxiety of the Advent season does not mean that we doubt whether Christmas will be celebrated on the right date. What it does mean, though, is that we are afraid that the message will not be heard by us and ours, that the decisive birth will be noticed only in passing.

Every step means changing, being changed on the way to the Lord, participating in His transformation. Ultimately, the Mass becomes a symbol of every single earthly path; it becomes the path from today to tomorrow, from earth to heaven.

Trinitatis. The progression of feasts up until now in the Church year comes to a stop with Trinity Sunday, after having been heightened a final but unprecedented time beyond anything conceivable. The conceptual has found its end; it has been lost in what is shoreless, not by having been dissolved in it, but by becoming the boundless expanse itself. Until now, understanding was always able to embrace love; even though grace exceeded every expectation, it was always still somehow conceivable, often even tangible. Now it exceeds every dimension; it has become unanalyzable and, so, is no longer explicable either. It has passed into the Trinity. In doing that, it has burst the framework; it has become both picture and frame at the same time.

All too often souls do not linger where the Lord's Incarnation is at its most complete: in their neighbor or in the Eucharist.

John says to us: little children, my little children. Oh, if only we could also tell you that we want to take you by the hand and lead you to the Father like little children, serving you just as one does little children. How close to you we would be then. But we have become accustomed to consider you as adults; how difficult we make the path for you by our unreasonableness. Let us relearn how to say: little children, my little children.

Christ's last abandonment is often the greatest for Him precisely among those who love Him; for they love Him somehow "by the book"—and so they do not want to see Him.

God, You know how much we love Your "child";[2] but we really only love it because it is Your child that You have entrusted to us. But please: let it be born only on condition that it does not love You "by the book". Let Your love for it and its love for You remain alive; do not let this love perish from our incompetence; draw our most intense love precisely out of our inability.

The reaction that our children's mistakes provoke among others is often more embarrassing to us than the mistakes themselves; a sign, perhaps, of how little free of vanity we still are.

[2] The community Adrienne was to found.

V

With my eyes I see everything humanly. Lord, make me blind, so that I will be forced to entrust everything to Your eyes.

The ability to suffer and the ability to love are one.

My God, allow me to suffer and to love, indistinguishably, when You will, as much as You will.

Suffering without faith would be like love without hope.

In order to have a meaning, suffering must be endured; flight is no way to deal with it. Sedatives and diversionary tactics become pointless here, because they diminish the power of suffering.

When, for the space of a moment, fate reflects the Absolute, man often tries to pray; prayer should ease his suffering, and so it acquires a definite task. Things are different when God imparts something of His absoluteness to prayer. In that case, suffering may become an absolute demand, the one consequence of a prayer of self-offering.

To try to see a path in the midst of suffering would already be to measure something, to settle down; the temptation to do that is so great that total darkness is just barely enough to avert it.

The night is there to remind you of your powerlessness; bless the darkness, for it shows you the Lord.

When you suffer, you cannot go wrong. Because you leave the action to God then, because you surrender to Him everything you bear in His name, the effect is much surer than if you had handled things yourself.

You do not need to meet the Lord if you are in Him.

You do not really experience what solitude is until the Lord invites you to enter into His solitude and to share it with Him. But do not be surprised if at just that point you do not meet Him and have to walk the path without Him.

Whoever has once known real solitude will encounter it again and again.

Total solitude is always a pure gift; it is never something we choose for ourselves. It has never occurred to anyone just to part with the Lord out of love for Him, to stay waiting forever where there is no more presence, no Host to be seen, no Communion to receive. Solitude in the monastery really is not solitude, but rather living, grace-filled proximity. No cell is far from the tabernacle, no praying soul is deprived of the Eucharist.

If you have love, then say you do—though, if you say you do, then you really do not.

Sacrifices are the most tender flowers; they lose their fragrance as soon as you speak of them.

As a symbol the Lord took the vertical line and the horizontal line and combined them into a single structure with ends and a middle. The Cross, nailed together by the sinner as a sign of the redemption and borne by the Son as the price of supreme humiliation, now contains nothing but paradoxes. This explains why the last shall be first and why the more I have sinned, the more I will be forgiven; and why, when I begin to love, I realize that I have no capacity for love; and why, when I try to understand something of God, I realize clearly that I do not understand anything; and why everything is light because He appears to us precisely as dark.

Mist is often the only thing that can tell of the sun.

Every rainfall refreshes; the Lord's rainfall, however, kindles thirst in the first place.

There is a path on which all bridges have been blown up; grace then emerges right on the brink of the abyss.

If you had never drunk, you could not give thirst a name.

Faith and suffering as a unity in God; if a person could believe like the Son, he would also receive His suffering, since He Himself unites both in Himself and is Himself this unity as Word.

You have palpably separated joy and suffering for us; for You, they flow into each other and are barely distinguishable. We could not bear this escalation, this simultaneity of being at the top and at the bottom. But instead of thanks, all You hear is our complaints about the rhythm of the alternation between the two.

VI

Holiness would be: being like a puddle that wholly reflects a golden cloud. You see neither the mud nor the water in the puddle, only the light it serves, and without it, you would not once see the golden cloud.

Nothing clings more tenaciously to the saints than the dust of our humanity; it would take a steady, powerful wind to free them from it, to restore to them the complete clarity and splendor that is theirs; this wind could only be their own spirit, shared with the Church and endowed with the force of their living prayer.

The personalities of the saints are so various that before we honor them we should ask them how to show them veneration.

The power of God fills the saints, but they often feel it as an infinite weakness.

More and more the impression that the entire Sermon on the Mount is addressed to religious, even more: that it was pronounced in order to call, and also to form, religious down through the centuries.

Lord, give us a monastery in which every communion is offered up to *You*, every penitential exercise is performed with *You* in mind. Let those who intend to walk the way of perfection do it only for love of *You*. Let every climb upward be a sinking downward to You in humiliation and disgrace; let the only calculation be: to be prodigal, and nothing else. Lord, let the direction in this monastery be toward a catastrophic being lost in You. Grant it, Lord: we are so often reticent about our petitions, because we do not want to put any obstacle in Your way. But You did say: Ask, and it will be given to you.

In turning Mary away in the Gospel, the Son also gives her spiritual motherhood, for who believes more strongly than she?

Mary spoke very little. The silence in which she concealed herself so well reveals the Son's word all the better. She lets *Him* speak, and yet in His Word hers is also hidden.

Mary and her Son walk side by side in such a way that there is always room for both; there is never any need for one or the other to step aside.

Because the only thing I can do is love, I turn my eyes to you sinners, and all I can think of is the birth of my Son, for which I thank you. At the same time, I do not see my path or suffering, but only His future path. If it were not for your sin, I would not have had to say my *fiat*,[1] and so I would have been left without Him. For His sake, then, I can look away from Him and look gratefully upon you. And by doing that I can give Him wholly to you and, so, to the Father, that the Word might be fulfilled.

He came in order to forgive as savior and judge, to give the gift of His grace, to walk the path of suffering, and to take your sins upon Himself. But I can only love, dwell in Him; and because I have received the divine Son through you sinners, on your account, I can love you in God even as the sinners you are.

Through you I love Him, and through Him I love you.

[1] "Let it be done."—TRANS.

VII

Folded hands signify being bound; even more, it seems to me: between folded hands there is no more room for anything else—even for something that is just coming into being. But when the hands separate again after prayer, perhaps, Lord, You can entrust them with something, as a proof that everything comes from You.

Our petitionary prayer is often so stormy that we can hardly formulate it, and it fills us in such a way that we can no longer divide, separate, and pronounce it; it just stands before You, formless and overflowing; we leave it entirely in Your hands, and it may even contain what You wish to grant.

God's entire love is needed for Him to hear the stammered word "father" out of all our prayer.

You always help with prayer; the Our Father is Your gift to us; when we want to use other words, You put them in our mouth. There are also the prayers of the saints; we see clearly in them that they come from You.

Your best is something you can only offer to God naked, just as you are; your fellowmen accept it only when it is clothed in mediocrity.

For business reasons, we send respectful greetings to people who we know exist only because their names appear in our address book; that is part of our routine, it does not strike us as at all out of the ordinary. Do we not also use words that have become empty of any concepts when we talk with the Lord? Do we still seek to be true before God, and do we let Him fill up our stammering with His Spirit?

A prayer never becomes a dialogue; for either I speak and so do not listen, or God speaks and I am allowed to fall dumb and remain blissfully silent. And in fact, the way every Word of God appears—not sounds— is designed to make us blissful, even when it demands too much from us and uses us up.

Souls who try to live entirely in God experience the divine presence even in the smallest details of everyday life.

If two people are silent together, it is always possible that at least one of them is praying at that very moment.

It is impossible for you to pray without also being right with God; that would be like carrying on a conversation while refusing to give your partner a chance to answer; a monologue, however, is never a prayer.

Christian penance is a reservoir from which prayer can continually draw fresh energy.

Every prayer is like a vessel to which we ourselves can give some sort of shape. What fills the vessel, however, is always supposed to be an encounter with God, and He alone can give this encounter a shape.

Consolation can open the way to love and generate a return gift out of the one that has been given.

Contemplation can be compared to an echo. One must not be standing too far away, and yet one must preserve a certain reverential distance; that is the only way God's answer can be discerned.

Vocal prayer often seeks, even without knowing it, exactly what contemplative prayer finds.

If there were regular degrees of prayer, God would thus allow himself to be grasped, to be prayed for, stage by stage.

We can only plan things that take place outside of us; what occurs inside of us is gift.

Transfiguration means insight into one's own powerlessness; no longer I, but You; and if by "You" in the full sense we mean God, then active transfiguration gives way to being passively transfigured. Active transfiguration belongs to me and has a human savor; in the passive, however, the I is forgotten and the turn to the better has come.

So long as I efface myself, a part of myself remains standing, preoccupied with myself, precisely with the activity of effacing. Radical effacement can happen only if God does it.

It is better to let oneself be found by God than to seek Him.

In order to receive an answer from God, one need only hearken, not ask.

So long as I live in my prayer, I am the one who gives it its duration and shape; if God lives in it, however, then He is the one who takes over the whole of it.

My supreme possession, Lord, is You; I offer You up to the Father, I give You to Him.

Lord, I want to be Yours; so much Yours that nothing of me is left over. You have given all to me; please, take it all back, totally, as if it had never ceased being Yours; use it as You use what is Yours, anonymously and prodigally. Scatter it. Scatter me.

The "always now" of eternity is much more comparable to our yesterday or our tomorrow than to our today.

To belong only to God. . . . To have an inkling of that would be bliss; to know it, death.

VIII

Death is God's invention that finally prevents the sinner from resisting His grace.

Life should increasingly become a Christian preparation for death. Not, say, by letting the thought of death increasingly preoccupy our minds, but by preparing ourselves with increasing intensity to appear before the Lord, knowing how glorious His grace is at the moment of death.

Death is precisely the opposite of every "Know thyself." For what is shown and given in death comes so totally from God and from the *Una Sancta*[1] that the dying person can surrender himself totally as well, not into the "*in manus Tuas*"[2] of the Cross, but into the Lord's new gift of the "*in manus Tuas*" of the redemption, the immediate redemption from temporal life into eternal life.

The fulfillment of life consists in the fact that at the moment of death it shrivels to nothing, leaving all the room to the new life.

[1] "One Holy."—TRANS.
[2] "Into Your hands."—TRANS.

Every life receives an immeasurable value by its survival. Hence the Christian's reverence for every human life, which, on account of its surviving, is supremely worth being lived.

I cannot lose my dead. What they give me is often the very thing that makes today alive for me.

To fear death means to shift it completely into the temporal and to forget the power of the sacraments that ferry us over to the other side, that prepare and purify us. To know death, by contrast, means to know that God remains the eternal giver and that out of a kind of yearning He already uses the moment we pass over to manifest His presence more clearly.

By means of death, I was shown in a new way how absolutely contrary to God suicide is. The Church and the Lord meet in the dying person at the hour appointed by God; those who decide for themselves the hour in which they die prevent this meeting.

It is as if this encounter between the Lord and the Church occurred in a mutual obedience; the dying person is simply taken into the midst of it so that it can be accomplished in him; as this happens, his obedience is not just presupposed, but, in a certain sense, is actually performed by the Church in the Lord.

The grace of baptism and the grace of the last sacraments closely resemble each other; both mediate a new birth, the one into temporal life, the other into eternal life. The first gives the strength to overcome with the Lord; the second gives the certainty that the Lord has overcome and that He has done so with and through His Church in a unity whose mysteries the Lord's eyes alone fully encompass. Of course, it is precisely through its mysteriousness that this unity is meant to give the Church a certain visibility in the Lord.

The last sacraments contain a sort of real presence of the otherwise—alas—so invisible Church, which here, though, becomes absolutely evident.

There are hard deaths and easy deaths; but if the sacraments could somehow be administered to every dying person in a way that enabled him to realize their true meaning, the consummation of every dying would be a redemption already in life.

When the whole of one's past life disappears, as it were, before death, this means it has fulfilled its entire purpose: of having led to God: through Him, in Him, and, what is best of all, *to* Him.

Just as in the clearest confession one sin committed is inseparable from every other sin, what the sacrament of extreme unction shows is that the anointing removes all of this together in its deep connection;

from now on, no part of existence is separable from any other.

The sacraments actually suspend so-called "death", because they suspend every equation; they open the gates to let the next life pour itself out into this one. This is almost a complete reversal of expectations: we do not need to cross painfully over to the other side; heaven is "brought" to us.

In death the main work lies before God. Seed to body, cadaver to resurrected body. Holy Saturday as the quintessence of all fruitfulness in solitude before God. Purgatory: decisive becoming toward God.

Purgatory. One perceives that time has passed there only by the intensity of one's sensations, by the nuance of one's feelings. When one's torment has intensified, then it is later; and, when it becomes intolerable, later still. In itself, the punishment does not increase; what increases is only the awareness of how just it is, of how true its substance is, of how accurate its aim is. "I have spurned the Lord" can initially be a debatable assertion; it gradually gains in urgency until it becomes a gnawing certainty that eats into the soul. The only way to avoid it would be to flee; but the soul yearns for purification, which is why it cannot withdraw. It remains, delivered over to knowledge.

The first step in the fire, and it is perhaps the most painful one, is the realization of one's own sin. One is spared nothing there; one's knowledge has to be complete. Only then is it replaced by prayer, before finally being erased by the fulfillment of that prayer. The knowledge remains, but it is no longer painful, because sin loses its name and is no longer personal.

Nothing comes first, nothing comes last; rather, everything comes together. The knowledge of every single sin is simultaneous; although this knowledge does increase in depth, at the moment of the fire it starts everywhere, so that no particular sin of one's own stands out apart from the others; these others are equally one's own, too. Everyone contemplates his errors, is dismayed at their sum and even more at their common effect. Then he is oppressed by his lack of love, by the pain he has inflicted on God. Finally, he collapses under this very pain, requesting forgiveness for it. And now he is ready to suffer anything to expiate it and then to help others who may not yet acknowledge.

In the fire: The knowledge of the coming vision is extinguished; sin, along with its burdensome weight, is perfectly grasped, and it oppresses in its definitiveness. One is no longer enslaved to it, by any means, for it has been deprived of any allurement. But for that very reason it clings all the more tenaciously. Every attempt to liberate oneself only seems to tighten one's fetters even more. The experience of God is somehow near, and yet it is completely impossible. The search for faith becomes a torment, for there is no longer any hope for peace or for being found.

There is, though, one thing that remains or perhaps arises for the first time in the fire: prayer. And from now on it is the kind of prayer that rises up only against sin, against all sin, period—no longer only against one's own—because sin stands for Christ's suffering—then prayer is heard, accepted, and becomes liberation—not only from sin—but from all its bonds, and at the same time this means that the fire is at an end. The way can be long, but there is only this one exit.

The prayer that just now was still supplication becomes a song of praise; it accompanies the soul— the soul now purified through the fire—from the fire into heaven. No soul comes to Christ otherwise than praying.

The more that passes through our hands, the more we hope they will be empty when we appear before God.

IX

Every mystery that is penetrated along Christ's path conceals countless others within itself; the more you study it, the more mysterious the whole appears; conversely, everything is thus so clear for simple souls because they are ready from the beginning to accommodate all mysteries in themselves and do not wish to touch them.

God has given us everything; we do not know that until we give everything back to Him. And, once we are completely emptied out, we are still filled with what is always only His, so that we can never measure the greatness of His gifts.

There is only one way to defend yourself against God: totally surrender and hand over all the keys. Every treaty we might try to make with Him after that would, by its own logic, diminish the gift He has made us in His Son.

Lord, if Your severity toward me really is the sign of Your indulgence with others, then do not listen to my weariness and my sighs; do not spare Your severity; lavish it on me, whatever I may object to it.

And all these people on the street, on the bridge: the fog envelops them, puts them in a uniform, and they appear to you as priests, all of them clothed in the same black. You wish they were priests; you feel as if they were priests. But when you actually approach them, the fog parts for a moment, and you see them as they are, without priesthood and without an acknowledged mission. And then you realize: host and sacrament, host and renunciation are foreign to them. Fog and nightfall unite them, envelop them, as Your mantle would, Father, and they could all be brothers.

A flame of love seizes you now, penetrates you, becomes a torture under which your whole soul groans. You wish they were priests, and you offer yourself, you offer them as a holocaust. You will not be heard, but the flame consumes you, forces you to worship, and in your torment you offer these future priests, with the pain of all days.

To suffer in God is a form of love. Every suffering is possibility—a deepened, recognizable, open possibility of love, of reciprocity. Somehow, once the books are balanced, once God no longer considers one's sufferings as an obligation, as an expiation for one's own sin, pain and agony become paths open to Him. From that point on, suffering has only one meaning:

love offered. Of course, not all are caught, for God chooses. He does offer Himself to all, though.

To persevere with spirit means constant development for man, even if this is only an unfolding into the act of remaining.

Your friends praise your virtue; your family speaks of your faults.

It is hard in this noisy, cold, indifferent train to imagine that one is traveling for God, that one is resolved to live for Him alone, in dialogue with Him.

The sword has two edges and cuts both ways. Sometimes it is love and yearning, sometimes it is despair, the wretchedness of sin. But it does not remain in mere alternation. Every step is contact, every contact becomes fuller knowledge of the whole, summing up and summed up.

To grasp that the suffering of others can be volitional, can be deserved, is a terrible experience. It is one of the most shattering things that can move a heart. Beyond that, there is only a greater, more complete self-offering, even if it cannot alleviate that very suffering of the other.

Out of the restlessness of our nights You build the repose of our days; and in the night You empty us so completely that during the day we can squander our fullness. This makes it plain: only You are . . . , and we have long since ceased. And that is Your greatest gift.

Every distance from You, Lord, makes us cry out for Your nearness; but if we stand by Your fire, about to be caught by it, we clamor loudly for cool refreshment. And this eternal longing for what we do not possess, this urgency about precisely what is not attainable, this breathless inward seesaw, being thrown to and fro, is supposed at every moment to look outwardly like perfect rest in You. Lord, help us to do that; we are unworthy, but let us fulfill the task nonetheless.

Annihilate me, Lord. And if You are pleased to restore me, so that I can somehow be useful to You, then only on one condition: that I no longer know myself and finally stop seeking myself.

Christ became so weak that He was able to carry the whole world; and we become so strong that we can only be carried.

And if I cannot conquer myself, Lord, then You conquer me.

On the Cross the Lord's arms are opened more widely than ever before; they grow stiff from sheer openness, but they can longer close into an embrace.

I shed tears for anguish of heart, but my cry also meant: More, Lord, if it is Your will and I can bear it.

Intra tua vulnera absconde me:[1] because on the Cross You can no longer embrace with Your arms, I have to take refuge where it is still possible to be embraced.

Nihil divinum mihi alienum;[2] but when it gets to the point that you cannot even kneel any more, how strange that is!

If I have a bit of courage, then at the decisive moment it is always *it* that grabs *me*, rather than the other way around.

Claudel's Violaine. To give over what is dead to the saint, so that she can bring it back to life, even more: so that she can feed it. The saint complies by virtue of her readiness. Mara possesses the secret that comes true in Violaine and exists for Mara. *Suis-je un lépreux?*[3]

---

[1] "Within Your wounds hide me."—TRANS.
[2] "Nothing divine is alien to me."—TRANS.
[3] "Am I a leper?"—TRANS.

Pierre de Craon can accomplish his task because *she* renounces.

In the end, there is no restriction on my right to dispense as much spiritual advice to my patients as seems right to me. It even belongs to my method of treatment. I can call this advice objective, since it is inseparable from the other means I employ to heal; it is thus a part of my method of treatment. Just as I do not let my patient or those around him prescribe the choice of medicines, so do I not allow myself to be given instructions in my other consultations and conversations. The patient can choose his doctor, but the doctor, too, has freedom in his office.

Sometimes a real awareness of the mission and almost every time the agonizing fear that I could trample it to pieces, that I could hinder God in His plans. A serious plea: As much suffering as You will, Lord, if only something of Your will can be done.

Every kick received may allow the destruction of something that can then bear fruit somewhere else. Often the need to show others how easy pure renunciation is through the Lord's grace.

Catholicism in the eyes of the diaspora: Is a Catholic dumb? "Only a Catholic can be so dumb!" Is he smart? Then maybe he is not really a Catholic but is only pretending to be. Is he actually a convert? He probably knew of no other way to get himself talked about.

Lord, we are tired of being grownups. Let us become children. Take from us everything we thought we had to acquire, deprive us of all knowledge, cloud our knowing, and upset our calculation. Instead of a multitude of words and an infinity of names, give us love. Your love, Lord, not our love.

Lord, let me die as a seed in You so thoroughly that I may bear fruit in your crop anonymously.

Between us and the world stands solitude; however close the world may be, solitude is even closer, and its imperviousness becomes all the more noticeable, the more the world presses in. This explains a lot, if not everything. In today's conversation—when I realize: the other may be about to stumble onto this place of solitude—I have to take charge, regardless of how tired I am, lest he steer it to the point where solitude, being injured, might recoil because of the excessive pain.

Because I lack great things, I have an even more binding obligation to persevere in little things.

In everything *I* do, my role is always that of the insignificant extra. There is only one thing I must not do: prevent or conceal what You do.

The emergence of action out of contemplation has perhaps never been so evident as in the Virgin Mary's "*Fiat mihi secundum Verbum tuum.*"[4] We see in these words the inclination to say Yes and how the consequences unfold out of that Yes like an avalanche—though the unfolding is left entirely to God's power, and its flow is henceforth only suffered passively. It can no longer be influenced. Some elections are irrevocable; crossroads that one comes to afterward are only a sign that there is no turning back. They seem to offer a further possibility of decision, but the most vehement No would only be judged as if it were a weak Yes.

Your gentleness surrounds us so palpably, Mother; allow it to spread out completely to others. You let us experience many things we are glad to linger over, even though we know that we should not stockpile them for ourselves. Switch us off as far as possible, so that we can faithfully pass on what, after all, is ordained for Your other children. Grant Your grace, so that, living in it, we may do nothing but disperse it.

Only when I am hard pressed and encompassed by an ultimate weakness do I sense the magnitude of Your strength. Lord, if there is no other means to bind us irrevocably to You, let us live hard pressed until the end: hard pressed by our imperfection and our

[4] "Let it be to me according to Your word."—Trans.

incapacity; but take our refusal from us, Lord. Let it fade beyond hearing, let it perhaps become mute in anguish and affliction. And if even that still is not enough to suffocate it completely, at least let it become lifeless by refusing to hear it. Then we will no longer be mere obstacles to You, and what You have awakened will have a chance to develop.

Prayer. Accompany us, O God, from one hour to the next throughout this day. You know that we seek You on awakening, promising You to do Your will, but that afterward we get caught up in things that are not You. My God, do not abandon us, do not allow us to do our will, but solely a little part of Yours. My God, do not abandon us, do not allow us to act instead of You. My God, do not abandon us, but let every word we pronounce today be a stammering toward You; let it become a prayer. Help those who are entrusted to us like a petition, like a testimony of Your goodness. My God, do not abandon us!

To be crumbled totally into You, so that the resulting host may present You alone. So that You may be fully presented in every crumb we distribute. To pray that Your grace, Lord, may give our action an efficacious presence.

The questions that the pure person might ask would always be misunderstood.

Those who work in the light do not need to drag their work into the spotlight.

There are so many beautiful things that can be said about silence; the most beautiful of them all, however, can only be kept quiet.

Lord, let it grow quiet in my heart. Dampen the remaining echoes of my everyday business, of what is not Yours. Let silence fall, so that Your voice may henceforth be all that can be heard, so distinctly that from prayer I can then take it with me into my everyday life and so make my everyday life a prayer. From that moment on, though, my voice should say only Your words.

Lord, let our life become a candle that burns for You. Light it, so that You can have light or warmth to delight in, or even just so it smells a little like wax . . .

Word and silence possess the same transparency in the Lord, for He is not only the Father's Word. He signifies just as much the Father's silence.

Greatness often consists in surrender to littleness; God alone decides whether that surrender must remain there.

At Christ's birth Mary was the symbol of the holy vessel that merely contains; and yet she did nourish the Child with her own milk.

What is in us is greater than we are; thus the content is bigger than the vessel. Whether the vessel cracks in the enterprise or merely overflows is a matter of indifference. Only one thing matters: the tidings we bear must go forward.[5]

---

[5] The last two aphorisms were cited in my collection of aphorisms, *Das Weizenkorn*, 2nd ed. (Eisiedeln, 1953), 107, 111; English edition: *The Grain of Wheat: Aphorisms*, trans. Erasmo Leiva-Merikakis (San Francisco: Ignatius Press, 1995), 121, 127

New Lumina

I

We must believe. We must pray. We must love. Symbols are not enough, everything must become reality; the individual's act is meant to be everyone's act. Surrender without looking back, without weighing the options. What you have received remains formless until you hand it on. We usually do not renounce until something is taken away from us. That is no renunciation, for renunciation is demanded as an autonomous act.

Je veux tout.[1] We, too, want surrender in its totality, love in its totality, *implacable* faith in its totality.

Fiat. Who says *fiat* anymore today? And if they do, then *fiat* what?

My love, the Lord said, is something I can only lavish prodigally; it is immeasurable; I can in no way divide it up in order to pass it on. You, with your small love, divide it and then pass it on, thimbleful by thimbleful. But with the great, the true, the one and only love, one must not act so. Maybe you need

[1] "I want everything."—TRANS.

to lose sight of your love, to learn to give your love away. Then it might be, when you spend your little bit of love without calculating, you would suddenly receive My love to lavish. Then your poor, pitiful love would turn into my love, into Christian love. That might happen.

That is what the Lord said. And then He lavished His love on all those who yearned for it, and on others, too. And He had so much love to dispense that He even poured out the love that was simply waiting there perhaps for someone to come who had need of precisely that.

We stood on the wayside, breathless. We would have gladly given away our love too; it seemed to us, though, as if the Lord wanted to wait until we were at a point where we could take part peacefully. And yet He seemed to be saying: I cannot wait, because even when it works within the bounds of time My love knows no calculation. The point is simply this: to love, now, totally.

September 8, 1942

For the believer, the Lord's grace can turn every period of waiting into a time of fulfilling expectation.

In people who truly believe, the un-catholic can no longer exist alongside the catholic; everything that tends to compromise melts away; for them, there is no longer any such thing as a transitory moment.

In dealing with an illness, the doctor counts above all on the patient's strength and constitution. He most often assesses an accident, however, in terms of the impact of external forces. In the Church, converts would perhaps above all be counted among the accident victims.

I would love to be able to point to a conversion that was not a result of misfortune, misunderstanding, or feelings of inferiority, but that flowed from an immediate attraction by God and shot straight up to Him like an arrow.

If the Lord permits it, an efficacious action in Him can be just as much a symbol of rest as it is of work.

Consider this: solitude in the diaspora. Can you bear the idea of being silently mocked by everyone around you? One consequence is that the Church will look on you as just another soul and will not give you the love that you particularly lack right now, because there is so much of the all-too-human in it. Do you realize that the reputation for eccentricity will precede you everywhere? Sensitivity and touchiness will of course be increased over the long haul. Carry your cross not without tears.

ca. 1942

As, for example, being rich obliges, so does being Catholic. You notice that especially on All Souls;

disposition over Purgatory = an administrative pur-
view. No stinginess!

The assurance of what IS; not through intuition, not
through knowledge, but simply because you SEE it.

We were afraid of missing everything and not suffering; but He has not forgotten us and has allowed us to
suffer and to feel the pain more acutely on account of
the silence He enjoined. And He has revealed suffering to us everywhere, far and near, where we knew
it would be and where we did not suspect it.

Love and suffering are so close to each other. The
Lord gives us His great commandment to love our
neighbor at the moment when suffering, His suffering, begins and at once proves to be inexorable.
How could we have understood His pain without
His commandment to love, since His pain flows from
love, just as it flows from Him?

The two things share a point where they inter-
sect. You rarely meet this point in an individual, even
more rarely in a whole people. It is undeniably cutting right through France just now.

We have suffered; will we know how to love, just
as Christ teaches us to, with nothing in our hands but
the beginning of His suffering for all, for each one
of us without measure? We, too, have empty hands,
empty of the tiniest offering that is not ourselves. At
the same time, though, they are full of what Christ

bestows on us. They are full of what He pours out in us so that we will pour it out in our turn, without spilling any of it: His love.

1942

To surmount difficulties without wanting to resolve them at any price.

There is so much considerateness in fog; it brings close objects even closer by enveloping us together with them. It gives mellowness to distant objects, and this mellowness slowly enfolds, not penetrated by what is harsh, but at most only interrupted.

Uncertainty in life; and yet for what is essential there is just one way.

The narrower the way, the more dangerous it is to stumble.

I do not want to drag anyone with me into my destruction, but, my God, I do want to take the path You have marked out for me, trustingly, knowing that it ends in the abyss itself. And if I do fall and my body, hurled through the void, is shattered, You will allow my cry to be transformed into thanksgiving.

The demand to be understood—"It is different"—Therein lies the hope of their comprehension—of a distance between "it is so" and "it is different", hence, a possibility of a comparison.

We cannot, not any longer at all. But *You* can. You alone.

The surprise that after a night like this there is a morning—tiptoe through the night.

A truth may not be a truth at all, but a death is a death.

Thierry Maulnier

Killed *by* the truth, in other words: by the fact that Christianity is not an illusion.

We love life only when we love death.

The person who rings the bells does not march along in the procession.

II

What are you? Where am I? Love does not separate; the Spirit scatters it. Where is God in the Three? In all Three!

The trinitarian vows, the trinitarian exchange like a religious order: the binding of each one in every other.

Every Christian mystery forces us to think: It is greater than I thought.

God is not like a number that can be plugged into any random equation, and His operation cannot be worked out by mathematical means.

The soul's life is rooted in the fact that from all eternity it has lain in God's intention. God's intention is trinitarian: What could be more alive? Thanks to this life, God can actualize His intention out of nothing.

What the Lord exemplifies to us are not new properties. Rather, He exemplifies properties of the Trinity in a human way.

In our voluntary solitude there is always a certain superiority. Not in His.

Every Christian renunciation, of whatever kind it may be, means saying Yes to something bigger and more authentic.

Those who wait for the Lord are sure of His presence; to prepare one's heart for Him is already to possess Him.

In the serpent there was a will to understand everything. But the Trinity cannot be understood that way, with our will.

Beforehand, I feel ready for everything I love; I feel that every step forward will be a conquest. Every repeated movement becomes a new discovery, not just something relearned, but a true gift. Beforehand, I experience the power to see my whole being expand. Being wrapped in bandages is less confining; every bandage that drops off will mean a little newly won freedom, with undreamed-of charm, as part of a forgotten treasure, until the day when I arrive at almost exactly the same point I have reached today. Then disappointment will set in. And this disappointment, which has long been my companion, will recapture me in its movement, which keeps getting narrower. Then I understand once and for all that freedom is not of this world; there is no freedom here. It is always just transitory, awakened by an ever-increasing thirst. And this thirst becomes intolerable by its very nature.

It is our intensifying need for God, and it contains obedience and subjection: the Eucharist calls for more Eucharist, and our supreme freedom lies in the words "Thy will be done." Will we be worthy of this perfect freedom of the children?

July 7, 1942

Lord, do not let us live without mystery.

III

Those who believe they know God but ignore His Church name the Creator and forget His creature.

The Church is like the vision of God on earth distorted by our sin.

In creation, God made the finite in time and in space. The sacraments are creation in reverse, in the sense that they bring the infinite into the finite.

God does not need to wait for our death to let all of our preliminariness enter into His definitiveness. This definitiveness is not rigid.

Hope gives us the strength to wait. The inexorability of dogma makes our spirit malleable by allowing it to adapt itself, to open itself, to grow. Dogma does not close things off, for its content is immeasurable. Testimony of the faith and the experience of millions of people, fruit of their trust, of their inquiry.

If the Church's bodily surrender were correctly understood, there would be no more need for any prudery; bridal mysticism, too, would be totally pure.

The essence of the feminine lies in surrender; but woe to those who lose their way in their surrender, who do not stop before they have sold themselves.

Mass: this unstoppable drama of divine becoming, which becomes only in order to be distributed.

January 24, 1943

Anyone who supposes that there are three states of life in the Catholic Church misunderstands the Lord's words: "Let your Yes be Yes, and your No No", and adds a "maybe" that is nowhere to be found in Scripture.

Water and wine remain pure only so long as they are not mingled; the so-called "third state" in the Church can be compared to any imaginable mixture.

It is natural for love to invest the beloved with the rarest qualities; it is natural for marriage very quickly to divest him of them.

Admonitions to people in love are not heard.

What the man calls being "tired" after the act, withdrawing somehow into himself, the woman can experience as a sudden self-disgust. With both, there is in the end a kind of crisis of a little understood egoism that is connected directly with original sin.

Conjugal love is nourished by much friendship.

A universal law cannot be abolished by the tragedy of a particular case. Indissolubility of marriage.

A plea on behalf of life. The child's words have a meaning; when I rediscover this meaning in the Church's words, I know I am at home, in the midst of my childhood, despite my age.

Reflections on "Casti Connubii". Every death can mean, and probably does in fact mean, grace and therefore remains immeasurable for us, like the impact made by the death of an expectant mother on her family.

It could be that a fullness of grace is unfolded in the child and through his life that was intended only for him, but not for his mother. So long as this intention is hidden from us, we are not able to want to play destiny and to make life and death decisions in favor of one.

If, however, it is clear that both lives are in our hands as doctors, and that, if we failed to intervene, both of them would inevitably be lost, then it should be possible and permissible to save at least one of them. The few cases that actually occur should be clearly defined by an encyclical. Then the few lives saved by sacrifice would take their place alongside the very many lives saved by the encyclical and the fifth commandment.

But who am I to judge? No doubt competent people were involved in writing the encyclical, and, so long as I am one doctor among others, maybe I should try earnestly to believe in order to understand and thus risk replacing understanding with faith, and I should stay with that until I have a genuine chance to keep working on this question constructively in the Church—and only in her.

Every call to the consecrated life, in its genuineness, boils down to this: "You, follow me." But what about marriage?

Obedience is like our daily bread; it nourishes and strengthens us for the assumption of ever new tasks.

Through obedience even the small becomes great, since an obedient person lives solely by the love of the Lord.

A superior who will not risk assuming responsibility is like a sponge that cannot absorb any water (has no raison d'être).

There is an obedience of the body that begins precisely where the body is humiliated through some sort of penitential practice. This obedience resembles a total oblivion, because the will of the body, with perhaps keener vigilance than ever before, dares to try to insert itself into the will of the scourged Lord.

There is no psychology of obedience; the superior can, of course, be the channel of grace, but its form and content remain indeterminable, even for him. He is perfectly capable of assuming an effect with certainty, but not to want to determine it in advance. Grace is always of an ever-different nature. That is something that even the Son experiences in His obedience.

For sisters in the hospital:

There are only a few conversions that set us once and for all in movement toward God. For the most part, our self-gift remains incomplete. So we need to be able to renew it each day with an ever-greater readiness and humility. Imperceptibly, we accustom ourselves to a life that seems Christian to us because we have chosen it as such ourselves, but we do not know how to give this life back every morning, in fact, every minute. No matter where we are, we settle in, we acquire habits, skills almost. The new position, the new task, has humanly attractive sides; we get attached to them and lose sight of our primary goal: to forget ourselves, not just partially, but totally. There is a verse in Scripture that expresses this goal: "I live, but it is no longer I who lives; rather, Christ lives in me." All of a sudden, we remember the words, we wake up, and we try to recover the dynamic impulse that made us wish no longer to be ourselves, but to be anything, anywhere, so long as it was in God, in God alone.

To wear a uniform means in one way or another to carry a banner. What makes the uniform or the banner valuable is not the piece of material it is made of, but the meaning it represents, and that alone. Wearing a banner that says "I belong to Christ" demands the very depths of our being, and permanently, daily. What we represent, what we are, does not get its value from us; it comes from Christ and returns to Him. We should learn to humiliate ourselves, that is, to love deeply and wholly enough to eliminate once and for all the wish to be loved by our sick patients, by those around us, for our own sake, but to want instead to inspire in them the love we serve.

And precisely because that is not easy, the gift of self—which takes visible form when we think of others—must be a daily new consecration. It should be uncomfortable for us when someone accords us this or that advantage; it should at most serve to point the way to the Lord, in whose service it stands. And when we speak of our way of life, our work, then we should be talking, not about ourselves, but about the Lord, realizing that what we do exists only through Him. Let us not boast of any advantages; they exist only in Him, and He has loaned them to us so that we might glorify Him; these qualities come, as it were, only through us, and they have no purpose other than to point to Him.

Nurses know how to combat epidemics. Consecrated people need to combat the infectious diseases called routine and lukewarmness, for they kill the true love that we expect from them.

May God grant that neither the difficulties nor the monotony nor the joys of our profession will prevent us from ascending to Him and living in Him, turned perpetually toward Him.

Lord, give us the grace to offer You ever anew what You have given us. That is the only way for us unprofitable servants not to remain barren.

Will you be able to be non-conformists by being the sort of people who try to love?

Suffering is often what cannot be fought.

IV

What might have become of the Son if the Mother had not run the risk of giving her Yes to the whole adventure?

"Will call me blessed": the Mother's awareness of her own distinctiveness. The sense of inner elucidation enclosed within the sense of total surrender to God.

I could give over my mother to you only in a spiritual way; Jesus has given Mary over in a bodily way, too, as we see from the twofold direction of the "Fiat mihi"[1]—toward the spiritual and toward the bodily.

In the saints the feeling for balance. The density of their faith. Hatred of the vulgar. The idea of the more, but one that knows no "too much".

Madonna and child. Only in the picture does the child complement the Mother. But consider how things went with her afterward! Her renunciation be-

---

[1] "Let it be done to me."—TRANS.

gan already when she said "fiat mihi secundum verbum tuum."

Paul. When he boasts, he sees himself as the perfect Christian. When he reprimands himself, he sees himself as a member of the community. He is always both the spokesman for the Lord and an example that has been created by the Word.

He is the first one to grasp conceptually what the essence of Christianity is, and for that reason he may be the one who can best give us a living understanding of what following Christ means.

No development. He plays on himself, because he is an absolute instrument, but he knows neither humility nor pride, just necessity. Conversion for him means irrevocable commitment; the direction is given. And that is that. Mistakes? Of course, but they are not counted; they do not affect the work, for it is something given.

He is so totally the man who has been commissioned that he identifies himself completely with the goal to be reached. And that is why he draws a very clear line between himself and the community.

If he becomes more differentiated, it is for the sake of the community, which is diverse and thereby becomes more receptive. But he remains the paradigm of the original Christian; there is no going back for him, only going forward in the service of the mission. At the moment of his conversion he becomes a man sent.

He is the first one who *also* knows with his intellect what is going on, and this may explain why his grasp of things is not successive but sudden. He has to become a "teacher" right away, and so the teaching is just given to him. From the outset his struggle is external, one of mediating, giving; inner battles, struggles with truth, with faith, with progress on the path to perfection—his soul is spared all that.

He does not struggle, he possesses; a truth that so totally transcends him that he himself becomes the instrument on which he performs; for he has become an instrument, not only for Christ, but also for himself; he knows what a Christian looks like, with his sins and his dying; he cannot portray himself as a Christian, but only as the tool of the Master; he immediately uses what he endures as an instrument from which to coax new sounds for the community.

Life is a master that daily brands even the most mature person as an apprentice.

This is the tremendous thing, man: God gave you life. And, lest the gift should terrify you, He gave it to you as you lay sleeping on your mother's breast, and He only gradually awakened your senses and abilities in the games of childhood.

What the child reads penetrates him wholly, transforms him, and then leaves him standing interiorly breathless.

In terms of time there is nothing more irregular than childhood; it progresses by huge leaps and bounds, stands still for an eternity, then starts moving again with steps both slow and quick. If you try to lay hold of it, then you know with inevitable certainty: it is over.

Even in a believer, a heavy responsibility can generate something that bears a strong resemblance to a bad conscience. The "I cannot go on any more" is like a sin; it is probably a visible manifestation of original sin.

Before the Fall, Adam probably knew nothing of responsibility; his word would have been pure response.

By regarding your freedom as always threatened, you surrender it.

Chaos is the neutral part, the remainder, of creation, out of which man then draws the freedom to sin. A world without a remnant of chaos would be a world without personal freedom (measured in terms of the chaos, not in terms of God).

Bridled drives will send out warning signals.

Temptations. Cordis somnolentia,[2] against reverence for God's presence. Caution; do not trust too much to your own powers in order to devote yourself to what is more pleasant.

When it comes to insolence, the measure is measurable: how far can one go in order to have gone a bit too far.

Indiscretion may use more ingenious words than might ever occur to you. That does not change the fact that indiscretion and vulgarity are one and the same thing.

Words that fall under the burden of their own weight cannot be canceled. They fall by themselves, drill a hole, demand their appointed place. You cannot remove them, unless you cut into your own flesh and remove them along with it.

The simplest thing often seems incomprehensibly difficult to us, but only because we do not understand that it is embraced all around by love.

The word does not only create relations to living things; it creates their life as well.

Love that cannot endure the everyday is not authentic.

2 "Sleepiness of heart."—TRANS.

To love the forsaken more than the satisfied.

We let our dead become so immature!

Prayer of humility. Let me be silent, even with You; what we have to go through or suffer is unimportant; in fact it has no meaning until You bestow this meaning on it. So what is the point of clothing everything in our own words? It comes from You; You know it better than we do. Please bless it, let it do entirely what You intend it to, only that.

June 1, 1943

Life as   1. Birth: God.
            2. Having lived: Son.
            3. Death: Spirit, pure return.

Unity as personal flourishing of faith. 2 + 3: No one has ever seen God.

It is not a sweet phrase. Each of the words, even when they sound sweet—is meaning*ful*, but comes from a *sweet* youth.

V

Often the Lord does not initially expect us to believe; He surrounds us visibly with His love until we feel at ease in it. Only then does He cause faith to flow from us, though He does it in a way that makes us think this faith has its roots in us.

A field is not always there because a farmer was. Sometimes just the opposite is the case: the field, heavy with fruit, is there, and only then the farmer, who reaps the harvest.

Our intellect always refuses to accept love as given. But how, then, is our heart ever supposed to understand anything?

If you give God a lot, then your debt to Him increases to the point of immeasurability. If you give Him only a little, then you have probably received little as well. For what we give Him is always only a part of what we have received from Him. We can never offer Him anything that comes from us.

Receive. Receive rather than give, for the "thank you" evens everything out again.

Christ's word tears through every visibility in order to give us a glimpse into the mystery. God is spirit and so is not contained in the visible; better: is visible only through invisibility. Christ did not come in order to replace the bakers and the doctors.

When the Father gives His Son as Word, one of the implications of that for us is also this: every word we do not fill with what He intends is meaningless, worse than a lie.

Lord, teach me to pray in such a way that my prayer serves only the discernment and reinforcement of Your intentions and not the fulfillment of my human plans.

God takes from us not only all our superfluous thoughts about ourselves. He also takes from us what in the end is most superfluous: ourselves.

Do not let our prayer become an occasion of sin. Let us pray for spiritual things, not temporal ones.

When I was a Protestant, I prayed every day about what made me suffer or frightened me, but only seldom to say thanks. I also knew a certain habitual recollection, but it was not that of either contemplation or adoration. And about proximity to God in prayer, about offering sacrifices to Him in prayer, I had no idea.

Contemplation should be fed, but not disturbed; equipped, but not overstuffed. And if there is room in contemplation for my care, then let it be the Lord's care and only that.

As soon as you have faith, you know that every word you speak is addressed to God: to God the Creator, God the Giver, God the Helper, God the Judge.

Where do the clouds go? Are they messengers? Do the white ones bring pleasant things, and are the dark ones laden with difficult and gloomy things? A man who seesaws his way into heaven.

The one thing all our calculations with God have in common is that they never come out even. In fact, that is precisely what characterizes them.

Only what does not belong to the Lord is futile. The purpose and point of what does belong to Him are unlocked in Him, so how could they be thus futile? That said, every reflection on the usability of what belongs to Him would be futile, because it would not be contained in, or come from, Him.

It is the inevitable that we give to the Lord. We have a sore throat, or our clothing is shabby; since we cannot change either of these things, we say "We want to bear this for the Lord." But we know: the reason we give it is that we cannot do anything about it. Otherwise, we would take steps to change it, and then we would stand there, as we often have in the past, with empty hands. We would have nothing, really nothing, for the Lord.

Our neighbor is cold or hungry, or he suffers some injustice. In that case, we are prompt to do some good, this or that. We fetch something warm and nourishing from our provisions; perhaps, too, a good word is enough; we will find it. We want to guarantee that we will be thanked, because we think we have averted some person's suffering. And, after all, we are doing well; the help we have offered has not diminished our abundance.

But how would it be if the recollection of our good deed were to perish? If our help were to expect no thanks? If it were not a human being, but the Lord, this anonymous one, who needed us, along with all our abundance?

He can need us, all of us, without our noticing that He is demanding it. It can become a sacrifice. Take all that we have, all that we are, Lord, and squander it, without thanks, even on those who do not want it, perhaps precisely on them. And do not let us talk about sacrifice.

First mortification (measure), then contemplative vision. Memory, intellect, and will go together in contemplation. Will as the main thing. But *nihil voli-*

tum, quin præcognitum: You cannot will anything unless you have known it first.

The woman with the hemorrhage: "Who touched me?" To touch Him precisely so that a power goes out of Him. No slackness in contemplation: readiness.

In prayer one makes resolutions in order to carry them out. Hold fast to the motive, for the resolution was made reasonably, even when one forgets certain details afterward.

Meditation as the needle, the acts to be inspired as the thread.

Rest in contemplation: being baptized. Its goal: action.

Let yourself be totally penetrated. SPN:[1] Find what you seek. Do not use many words, the Lord says; use your intellect to avoid distraction.

Prayer is not an end in itself, but a means for service.

Sometimes God shows His closeness precisely by uncovering the distance.

Contemplation is participation in eternity. We anticipate what we will do eternally.

[1] *Sanctus Pater Noster* [our holy father]: Saint Ignatius.

Graces come through prayer (like children in marriage); fruitfulness, then, is immediately implied in contemplation.

Zeal and love wither without prayer; everything becomes lukewarm, and the consecrated life completely misses its point.

Thomas Aquinas: a religious without prayer is a soldier without weapons on the day of battle. Prayer is a reliable source of strength.

Prayer is the work of the Holy Spirit in us. Some of it is communicable, but most of it crosses over the threshold into mystery.

Our Father

Your Fatherhood did not stop when You created us; it remains our lifelong companion; it is not subject to randomness but is steady like nothing else. You were, are, and will remain: the Father, and we have the privilege of calling You that in simplicity and love. But at the same time, we include all the requests that a child, in whatever situation he finds himself, can bring before his father. We stammer, full of care, afraid that You might not understand; and we speak out, calmly, confidently, knowing that You are always ready to receive us, that You have time for all our concerns; and we cry with our last ounce of strength, and what we

want is so enormous that even that cry falls short of it. You remain the same, O Father. We want to have Your name always on our lips, but it is often smothered by everything that is not You, that is probably just us, us children of ingratitude and unreason. But You know how we are, You are in us, even when we refuse to recognize it. Your greatness, Your unity, fill what we like so much to explain with many words, although we do not have a clear view of it: our inmost being. And this inmost being, our ultimate I-hood, is what is united eternally with You through our voice, for it needs neither to seek nor to find. Despite all sin, it remains intact; despite all external doubts, it does not waver. In all certainty it is tentative and questioning, perhaps still foreign to us, because it consists almost too much of only what is most intimate, ultimately of what comes from You and goes to You, knowing just one word: Our Father.

Being Father, You give everything, and we receive everything. You do ask for an account, but there is never a final calculation: it goes on into Your love.